PHILOSOPHY NOTES

Paul Giamo

Highland Community College

ABOUT PHILOSOPHY

NINTH EDITION

Robert Paul Wolff

University of Massachusetts, Amherst

PEARSON

Prentice
Hall

Upper Saddle River, New Jersey 07458

© 2006 by PEARSON EDUCATION, INC.
Upper Saddle River, New Jersey 07458

10 9 8 7 6 5 4 3 2 1

ISBN 0-13-154196-X

Printed in the United States of America

Table of Contents

Preface

1. **How do I study and learn Philosophy?**

   From the Greek language **philos** ("love of") and **sophia** ("knowledge" or "wisdom") this question really says, "How do I learn how to love knowing things?"

2. **But what will I get out of this course?**

   That's up to you. But I suggest that if you want results, concentrate on taking the first steps to get them.

3. **What are those?**

   a) **Come to class**- Not only will you fail tests if you miss your professor's explanations of this difficult and abstract material, but you will also be unable to understand the interesting debates your classmates are conducting inside and outside of the classroom.

   b) **Ask questions**- That's any philosopher's first job. If you don't understand a viewpoint in philosophy (and no one understands everything about all of them) there's no better way to seek help. And if you have always wondered what the answers were to some of life's puzzling matters (such as "why do the innocent suffer evil?") the subject we label "Philosophy" is precisely the place (and has been for the last 2500 years) where you can pose and think about such mysteries.

   c) **Take good notes**- Nothing's worse than feeling lost in an over-packed lecture hall with 550-600 others! Let your notebook or laptop be packed as well. Pack it with:

       i)   **A summary of the views of each philosopher.** Make sure you know which author had which views and understand each one's point of view.

       ii)   **Original examples.** Think of your own life in light of the exciting ideas you'll read and hear about in class. Is there really a God? Are your opinions "original" or some mass-produced result of "society"? What is love? What happens when we die? Popular movies, comics, and your own adventures will fit in. There's plenty to journalize about!

       iii)   **The vocabulary of philosophy.** Every chapter will introduce new philosophical words for you. These are necessary to philosophy. Use the glossaries and other resources in the text to make up flash cards for each new term you come across. I am including vocabulary in the practice tests in this Study Guide.

   d) **Do not plagiarize**- Use your own words when writing essays. It is permissible to quote the textbook according to formatting guidelines that your instructor or institution will provide (ex: Chicago Manual of Style, MLA format, etc.). Read and quote the original philosophers and not just the explanatory comments by the author of the textbook. When you do, you will be asked to provide the source and number of the page you are quoting.

e) **Know the originals**- As with the relationship between Cobain/Nirvana and the rest of 90s "Grunge" rock, the original philosophers are the groundbreakers who say it first and (some would argue) best. You need to know both the original passage (though it will be tougher to read) and the explanatory summaries given by the author of the textbook. If you are in a larger section, I suggest you form small study groups (less than ten people) and/or utilize TAs if they are available.

4. How do I write the essays for this class?

A few basic tips:

- ✓ Use correct grammar.
- ✓ Use correct punctuation.
- ✓ Use correct spelling.
- ✓ Be logical and use thesis statements, topic sentences, and well-structured paragraphs.

5. Anything else I should know?

Something unique about philosophy is that it can be divisive. Equally good arguments and points can be made on each side of an issue. If you debate rationally and respect all opinions involved, you will find you can learn something from those with whom you disagree dramatically. Enjoy philosophy. This class can change your life and viewpoint if you allow it to, and if your professor is as excited about it as I am. No one can answer all of your questions, but any good instructor should be able to share with you why philosophy is personally important to him or her.

Chapter One: What Is Philosophy?

I. Terms for Review

Atomism: The cosmological theory which states that all objects are composed of invisible entities called atoms. Lucretius was a defender of this point of view.

Claim: Any statement presented as a truth, whether objective knowledge or subjective opinion.

Color Line: The difference of attitudes and treatments that exists between whites and people of color.

Cosmology: The study and explanation of the universe. The Milesians were among the first thinkers to embark on such a study.

Dialectical Method: A method used by Socrates of asking questions and critically analyzing answers as a way to arrive at propositions that can be accepted as true. Also known as the Socratic Method.

Dialogue: A literary style of writing involving two or more speakers who are engaged in a kind of question-and-answer session. Plato most frequently used this form of writing with Socrates as the major speaker.

Double Consciousness: The ability to see oneself inwardly and also as others see one from the outside.

Empiricism: The theory of knowledge which states that the original source of knowledge is from the senses (seeing, hearing, smelling, tasting and touching).

Epistemology: The branch of philosophy that studies the nature, sources and extent of human knowledge. The word is also used to refer to a person's theory of knowledge.

Irony: A literary method used by Socrates as a way of engaging people in debate or discussion. This use of irony requires two audiences and a double meaning to the speaker's statements. The first or superficial audience understands only the surface meaning of the statement, whereas the second or real audience understands both the superficial and real meaning of the statement.

Milesians: A term used to refer to the first three cosmological philosophers- Thales, Anaximander, and Anaximenes. Their hometown was the city-state of Miletus (located in what is now Turkey).

Objectivity: For any claim, the state of corresponding to independent reality external to the mere opinion of the speaker or writer.

Philosophy: From "philos (love of) and "sophia" (wisdom), literally the love of wisdom.

<u>Rationalism</u>: The theory of knowledge which states that the original source of knowledge is reason or the rational mind, which apprehends truth independently of the senses.

<u>Rationality</u>: Claims can be adequately supported by reasons, evidence and arguments.

<u>Socratic Method</u>: A method used by Socrates of asking questions and critically analyzing answers as a way to arrive at propositions that can be accepted as true. Exposing errors in the audience's or student's responses to his questions is a basic step in this method.

<u>Universality</u>: For any claim, the state of being applicable to everyone, in every place, at every time.

<u>Western Philosophy</u>: Tradition beginning in the eastern Mediterranean lands in the Sixth century B.C. which has had the greatest impact on Europe and the United States.

II. Practice Tests

Self-Test 1: Definitions/Fill-in

For each sentence below, fill in the blank(s) with the appropriate term(s) or phrase.

1) When Socrates tells the religious "prophet" Euthyphro that he feels Euthyphro is a wise man and has much to teach Socrates, he is using _____.

2) _____ has been marked by the exclusion of much of the philosophical writings of non-Western, African American, female and other marginalized social groups.

3) The statement "Baseball features a playing field with four bases and two foul lines called a diamond" is _____, while the statement "In my opinion, the Boston Red Sox is the world's best team!" is not.

4) When you go to your professor or TA's office to ask questions and learn more, the two of you are engaging in a _____.

5) _____ was the element that Thales thought the entire universe was composed of.

6) _____ is the systematic, critical evaluation of the way in which we judge, evaluate and act, with the aim of making ourselves wiser, more self-reflective and therefore better men and women.

7) One of Socrates' most famous quotes is that _____ is not worth living.

8) _____ was Socrates' best-known student, who formed the school of philosophy called the _____ of _____ in _____ B.C.

9) One of Socrates' four basic principles is that the principles by which men and women ought to live are _____.

10) Another one is that _____ lies within each of us, not in the stars, or tradition, or religious books, or the opinions of the masses.

11) According to the textbook, the Western philosophical principle of _____ statements as philosophical truths is doubtful.

12) The author of *About Philosophy's* experiences in the nation of _____ working to fight _____ led him to believe that our philosophical views are not wholly objective and/or universal.

13) Rather, the author argues that the philosophical concepts we use to interpret our experiences of the world are shaped and determined by _____ that we have made in our lives.

14) W.E.B. Dubois claimed that African Americans have a _____, being conscious of both the interior self and how that self was perceived by the outside world.

Self-Test 2: Multiple Choice

1) Instead of accepting the opinions and rulings of the Athenian leaders and majority of his time, Socrates chose to:

a) leave Athens and preach his philosophy elsewhere.
b) become a martyr for the cause of independent thinking.
c) write his thoughts in the form of plays called dialogues.
d) establish a school called the Academy in 388 B.C.

2) Socrates exposes true and correct knowledge in the Platonic dialogues. How ?

a) By questioning his students to expose their lack of knowledge of the real meaning of his statements.
b) By questioning opponents like Thrasymachus to expose their ignorance of his statements.
c) By questioning the gods.
d) a) and b)

3) In the dialogue, *Republic*, Socrates and his student Crito agree that wisdom is held by a few who are trained to question their own opinions. What does this claim imply about the nature of good government?

a) That "majority rule" may be ineffective because the majority do not hold wisdom.
b) That the wise are in the best position to govern.
c) That each person's opinion does not hold equal value.
d) All of the above.
e) None of the above.

4) The example found in your text of the snobbish stranger asking a small-town farmer for directions to the fastest way to the state capital is an example of:

a) dialogue, since the two are exchanging questions and answers.
b) philosophy, since the stranger seeks wisdom.
c) irony, since the stranger is the superficial or first audience.
d) None of the above.
e) Socratic double irony.

5) Socrates insists that he himself is ignorant because:

a) he likes to trick people.
b) true wisdom involves awareness of the limits of one's own viewpoint.
c) he has no great truth to teach any more than his opponent does.
d) a) and b)

6) The process of questioning and answering by which we gradually, step by step, reach a deeper and deeper insight into the principles of truth and goodness has come to be called the:

a) dialectical method.
b) Socratic method.
c) a) and b)
d) lecture format.

7) One of the original insights of Socratic or Platonic philosophy is that because the world of the senses is merely an appearance of the deeper, underlying invisible reality and that the superficial meaning of ironic statements is only the appearance of its deeper meaning, therefore:

a) language holds the facts like a bowl holds cereal.
b) truth is a useful grip on the world.
c) the structure of language mirrors the reality of the world.
d) The facts contain language like a water-balloon contains water.
e) a), c) and d)

8) Thrasymachus insists that:

a) justice involves the protection of the weak by the strong.
b) justice involves the strong making laws through which they define as "right" for their subjects whatever is in the interest of the strong.
c) justice involves the weak overthrowing the strong.
d) there is no justice.

9) Thrasymachus aggressively tries to defeat Socrates at his own game by:

a) overpowering his laws.
b) not listening to the philosopher.
c) waiting for Socrates to advance his own definition of justice.
d) challenging Socrates' definitions.

10) The first counterpoint that Socrates is able to advance against Thrasymachus is:

a) that the strong do not always overpower the "weak".
b) that philosophy involves questioning the definition of "justice".
c) that the strong could make a mistake and create a law that worked against their own interest.
d) Socrates loses the argument.

11) The conclusion that can be drawn from your correct choice of an answer to number 10 above is:

a) that because the powerful can make a law that would accidentally work against their own interest, the weak would then have to disobey it and it would be both just and unjust at the same time--an impossible example which shoots down Thrasymachus's argument for good.
b) that their conversation can't end because philosophy is always questioning.
c) since Socrates has lost, his philosophy is no longer "great" and Aristotle enters the scene.
d) none of the above.

12) Whether or not the universe began with a "big bang" or another such occurrence is an example of what kind of philosophical questioning?

a) biological
b) metaphysical
c) empirical
d) cosmological

13) Ancient Stoics believed that:

a) one rational order commanded and controlled the action of both humans and physical nature.
b) the earth was created by an interstellar big bang.
c) philosophical conversations cannot end because of the constant process of questions.
d) the universe was composed of water.

14) Epistemology is most clearly involved with the:

a) study of life sciences.
b) study of human nature.
c) study of speculative cosmology.
d) study of the theory of human knowledge.

15) A rationalist such as Rene Descartes believes that:

a) knowledge begins in the human senses: taste, touch, smell, etc.
b) knowledge can never be certain, so keep questioning
c) knowledge is a product purely of the human mind or reason

Self-Test 3: True/False

1) Generally speaking, the goals of Socratic philosophy, namely to become a better, more self-reflective individual oriented toward deeper values and less likely to make biased and superficial judgments, are quite similar to the goals of philosophy on the whole. T / F

2) Rationality is not thought of as the mind's ability to present reasons, evidence and support for one's own beliefs. T / F

3) Universal statements are thought to apply to people of all cultures and geographic locales, regardless of ethnic origin. T / F

4) Objective statements correspond or are true to the world external to their speaker or writer's point of view, as opposed to merely reflecting the speaker's opinion. T / F

5) There is an interrelationship between objectivity, universality and rationality. T / F

6) Kant's *Critique of Pure Reason* argues that our rational minds give us knowledge of the appearances out of which we construct a phenomenon of external reality. T / F

7) What your text refers to as the "Western philosophical tradition" has for a long time excluded the writings of people of color like W.E.B. Dubois. T / F

8) It is not the approach taken by the textbook to call appropriate attention to these writings so as to amend, or even call into question the received truths of the established tradition of "Western Philosophy." T / F

9) All British epistemologists of the 18th century gave their agreement to such racist statements as those cited from Hume. T / F

10) W.E.B. Dubois's challenge to his readers to recognize double-consciousness is comparable to the Socratic challenge the ancient philosopher made to the Athenians to recognize the difference between appearance and reality in their views of society, right and wrong, and justice. T / F

III. Essay Questions: For discussion and reflection

1) In terms of the knowledge you can glean from your companion CD texts by Plato including the Apology, the Crito, and the Republic for example, what specific values and ideas did Socrates stand for? Explain how his perspective on life would make the choice of death the only rational, morally consistent option for him.

2) Reread the dialogue between Thrasymachus and Socrates. Now move on to Chapter 6 on Social and Political Philosophy, especially the articles on affirmative action and the social, economic and other injustices in society. To what extent does Thrasymachus have a point--though it should not, does power make right?

3) Compare and contrast the double-irony used by Socrates to the double-consciousness discussed in Dubois. Do we, like Socrates, intend or create different meanings towards different "audiences" in our own lives, especially when dealing with injustices such as racism and other social inequalities? Can a Socratic questioning open us to the double-consciousness of appearance and reality that Dubois so eloquently shares?
Be sure to refer to *The Souls of Black Folk* from the Primary Source CD-ROM.

4) From your companion CD-ROM, how does David Hume offer a challenge to the usual relationships between ideas that we form in our minds in the selection titled *A Treatise of Human Nature*?

5) From your CD-ROM selection by Lucretius, *On the Nature of Things*, how does the appearance of motion in the atoms differ from the reality?

6) From Marcus Aurelius's *Meditations*, (found on *The Primary Source* CD-ROM), would Apatheia be of any use to us as we struggle with our feelings and conflicts caused by social injustices in our world?

7) What information does Kant share with us in the *Critique of Pure Reason* to shed light on how the mind learns and absorbs new knowledge?

IV. Lecture Companion

The following lecture note pages can be used to record your instructor's lectures and assignments for this chapter.

Chapter Two: Theory of Knowledge

I. Terms for Review

Categories: A term used by Immanuel Kant to refer to the concepts with which the mind is structured. The text describes the categories as rules "for holding thoughts together in the mind"

Cogito Argument: The argument by René Descartes that implied the certainty of his existence. The term "cogito" is derived from the Latin phrase cogito ergo sum, which means, "I think, therefore I am."

Empiricism: The theory of knowledge which claims that all knowledge is ultimately grounded in sense experience. For the empiricist, the primary source of knowledge is sense experience.

Epistemological Turn: A term used in your text to indicate the reversal of the order of priority of metaphysics and epistemology, where epistemology takes precedence over metaphysics.

Impressions: A term used by David Hume to denote the kind of perception which enters the mind "with most force and violence." The term "impression" refers to the content derived directly from sense experience.

Law of Contradiction: A law of logic that states that a proposition and its negation cannot both be true at the same time.

Law of the Excluded Middle: A law of logic that states that either a proposition is true or its negation is true.

Method of Doubt: A process used by René Descartes to discover which propositions could be known with certainty. Descartes doubted everything that could be doubted until he found something that was impossible to doubt.

Method of Inquiry: A process used by Descartes to find things out. The method of inquiry had four rules, the most important of which was to believe nothing unless you clearly and distinctly understood it to be true.

Objective: In accordance with reality.

Rationalism: The theory of knowledge that claims that all knowledge is ultimately grounded in reason. For the rationalist, the primary source of knowledge is reason.

Solipsism: An extreme philosophical theory that claims that only my mind exists and everything else is only an idea in my mind.

Subjective: Dependent upon the subject or a matter of opinion.

Truths of Fact: An expression used by Gottfried Leibniz to refer to the class of true claims based on the principle of sufficient reason.

Truths of Reason: An expression used by Gottfried Leibniz to refer to the class of true claims based on the laws of logic.

Unity of Consciousness: A term used by Immanuel Kant to refer to the unity of all thoughts, feelings, and beliefs etc. in a single consciousness.

Skepticism: Proponents of this view doubt that the knowledge we have achieved is absolute, and advocate a continued search for the truth.

II. Practice Tests

Self-Test 1: Definitions/Fill-in

For each sentence below, fill in the blank(s) with the appropriate term(s) or phrase.

1)_____ is the doctrine that no adequate justification can be given for any of our beliefs about our world, even those which we feel absolutely certain of, such as the "fact" that I have a body, that fire causes heat, or that the sun will rise tomorrow.

2) An extreme form of _____ which refuses to acknowledge the existence of anything outside of the subject's own mind is called_____.

3) Descartes' first rule of the practice of his method is to_____.

4) According to Descartes, the one thing one can never doubt is one's_____.

5) The Law of _____states that a statement and its contradictory statement cannot both be true at the same time.

6) The Law of _____states that for any statement, either it is true or its contradictory opposite is true.

7) According to Leibniz, the ultimate reason or fountainhead for all things was _____.

8) The tabula_____ states that the mind comes into life_____ like a _____, and is _____ upon by experience like a chalkboard by chalk.

9) Kant's Theory of the Unity of Consciousness states that the thoughts and perceptions of *your* or *my* mind are_____
_____.

10) David Hume's challenge to both rationalist and empiricist epistemologies is called _____.

Self-Test 2: Multiple Choice

1) Descartes' contribution to foundationalist epistemology is:

a) the tabula rasa.
b) the cogito ergo sum.
c) our senses can be deceived but we can still know things.
d) None of the above.

2) Descartes moves in his argument from the premise that all his senses can be deceived to the further premise that:

a) there is no true certain knowledge that the sun will rise tomorrow.
b) empirical data interpreted or put in logical categories of order by the rational mind constitutes a true or correct perspective.
c) the mind is a blank slate at birth.
d) in fact, the senses are being deceived by an evil force or "genius."

3) Descartes' method of not accepting the truth of a conclusion until one has established the truth of the premises from which the conclusion follows is called:

a) the method of categorizing.
b) the method of gathering data.
c) the method of doubt.
d) None of the above.

4) In the *Meditations*, Descartes argues that:

a) clarity and distinctness are the criteria of certainty.
b) the goodness of God proves that clarity and distinctness are adequate criteria of certainty.
c) the evils of capitalism guarantee that we are being deceived by our senses, as in the First Meditation.
d) All of the above.

5) Both Descartes and Leibniz agree that knowledge originates in:

a) the senses.
b) the external material world.
c) God.
d) the mind.

6) The foundation of Locke's empiricism is a theory best described as:

a) memory plus body equals self.
b) knowledge is based on the senses.
c) cogito ergo sum.
d) tabula rasa.

7) A defect or counterpoint in Locke's approach to knowledge is that there:

a) are no grounds for determining true or false memories when establishing a foundation for self-identity.
b) is no answer to the split between mind and body.
c) are no means for dealing with the fact that the senses can be deceived.
d) All of the above.
e) None of the above.

8) The word "cognitive" means:

a) relating to the impact of social forces upon society.
b) relating to personal experience re-cognized by persons.
c) relating to mental processes connected with understanding, the formulation of beliefs, and the acquisition of knowledge.
d) the basis for knowledge is in the mind.

9) John Searles' model of the Chinese room is intended to point out that:

a) mental processes connect with understanding, beliefs, knowledge, persons and society.
b) computers manipulate data according to formal programmed instructions without really understanding what they are doing.
c) computers can be thought of as intelligent.
d) the basis for knowledge is in the senses.
e) None of the above.

10) William James' model of truth was that:

a) true knowledge must exist in a unified self or consciousness.
b) truth consists not only of abstract verbal solutions but practical working plans.
c) truth comes to us from the senses.
d) All of the above.

Self-Test 3: True/False

1) Pragmatists seek the same sort of absolute certainty that Descartes did. T / F

2) Hume's system of knowledge uses the same basis for knowledge that Locke's did. T / F

3) According to Hume, all of our ideas are either straight copies of sense impressions or combinations and rearrangements of copies of sense impressions. T / F

4) Hume believes that because we cannot doubt simple ideas, we can only doubt complex ideas. T / F

5) Unity of consciousness is a basic part of Hume's theory but not of Kant's. T / F

6) For Descartes, clarity and distinctness are the basis for knowing an idea is true rather than false. T / F

7) For Hume, sensations or impressions can be divided into small, unified bits or items. T / F

8) Kantian theory involves no logical concepts such as space, time and the law of contradiction that we use to organize our perceptions. T / F

9) Leibniz has a basis for true knowledge different than Descartes'. T / F

10) Leibniz has a basis for true knowledge different than Locke's. T / F

III Essay Questions: For discussion and reflection

1) In his *Meditations*, found on your *Primary Source* CD-ROM, Descartes begins what philosophy scholars call the "epistemological turn" with a quest for what he calls "absolute certainty." Is it always worthwhile to seek such certainty? About what matters are you more certain, feelings or "hard facts"? Are there some matters you are clearly and distinctly certain of, but cannot properly put into words? So then how is human cognition different from information processing machines?

2) If all of what we know is completed shaped and determined by our backgrounds, education, and so forth, can an individual life have a freely chosen, unique and deeply motivating purpose?

3) Reread Kant's *Prolegomena to Any Future Metaphysics* to address the following question: How can humans have caused material changes in their lives and the world if concepts were simply appearances, like images on a movie screen?

4) Can any argument or system of knowledge which pragmatically works to cause change in the material world be rationally transferred without some sort of foundation or first

premise? If so, shouldn't all epistemologies ,even new ones, be called "foundationalist" ?
If not, how do you explain "common sense"?

5) In the study of culture, frequently some characters in movies, books, and the like are
analyzed as symbols, representations of other value-systems or interpretative
perspectives. How can the character Morpheus in the exciting and popular film *The
Matrix* be viewed as a symbol for Socrates and the role a philosophy instructor plays with
Neo as the philosophy student?

6) In *Monodology*, found on the *Primary Source* CD-ROM how does Leibniz introduce the
notion of infinite possibility?

IV. Lecture Companion

The following lecture note pages can be used to record your instructor's lectures and assignments for this chapter.

Chapter Three: Metaphysics and Philosophy of Mind

I. Terms for Review

Autonomous: Immanuel Kant argues that we are autonomous, meaning that we are free to obey laws that we discover through the use of our reason. Kant believed that we have free will.

Determinism: The theory that maintains that every event has a cause beyond human free choice. This view is also known as causal determinism.

Dualism: The metaphysical theory that claims that reality consists of both material entities (such as bodies) and nonmaterial entities (such as minds).

Free Will: The ability to choose to do some act without being caused to do it.

Idealism: The Mind-Body theory that everything in the universe is either minds or ideas in the minds (hence, idealism). Bodies, according to the idealist, are simply particular collections of ideas. Thus, a table is simply the interconnected set of all of the ideas- concepts, images, feels, sights, sounds, and so on.

Identity Theory: The theory that claims that states of consciousness are identical to brain states. For example, seeing is identical with certain neurons in your brain being stimulated.

Materialism: The metaphysical theory that claims that only material entities, such as bodies, are real or exist. Materialism denies the reality or existence of nonmaterial things.

Metaphysics: The branch of philosophy that studies such things as the nature of reality, the nature of being, and the nature of God.

Mind-Body Problem: The problem of explaining what kind of relationship exists between the body and the mind, or between physical events and mental events.

Scientific Materialism: A modern version of materialism defended by J.J.C. Smart. It states that the only things that exist are those things postulated by physics. According to scientific materialism, energy counts as matter. This kind of materialism implies a determinism in human nature if it cannot account for the reality of human free choice.

Self-Test 1: Definitions/Fill-in

For each sentence below, fill in the blank(s) with the appropriate term(s) or phrase.

1) From the Greek meaning _____ the physics, the term _____ means the study of the most_____ _____ of the nature of beings.

2) If I believe or think that physical objects in space are all that exist in the universe, I am a _____ist.

3) _____ is the belief or theory that there are two different kinds of things in the world–bodies and minds, or material and immaterial things, and neither can be reduced to or analyzed into the other.

4) Idealism is the theory that only _____ are real or exist.

5) Hobbes implies that human free will is simply a matter of _____ and aversions.

6) The counterpoint to the materialist explanation of the nature of human life is called the _____objection.

7) The "Mind-Body" problem is the problem of_____
_____.

8) _____ can exist by itself and does not need something else for its existence, as characteristics or properties do.

9) Descartes' theory of _____ _____ held that the physical and nonphysical realms of existence interact with each other.

10) Various _____ claim that every event that has a mental description has a physical description as well.

Self-Test 2: Multiple Choice

1) How many sorts of motions does Hobbes posit are peculiar to animals?

a) One: animal motion.
b) Two: the vital and the voluntary.
c) Three: materialistic, idealistic, dualistic.
d) Hobbes claims no types of motion are peculiar to animals.

2) For a materialist, voluntary motion gives persons the illusion of:

a) material force.
b) God.
c) Free Choice.
d) the self.

3) What we call "willing" or freely choosing or desiring some object outside the self, like food for example, is caused in Hobbes' thinking by:

a) atoms in the brain.
b) chemicals in the brain.
c) electricity causing consciousness in the brain.
d) consciousness causing electricity of the brain.

4) If materialism is correct in characterizing human consciousness as only physical phenomena, then androids can be thought of as:

a) designed by concepts that relate to reality.
b) designed by human beings using concepts they have created.
c) fully alive as human beings.
d) potential significant others.

5) The example of Gulliver using large and small dominoes to trick the Brobdingnagians illustrates:

a) determinism is an illusion caused by our inability to see the future, and a loss of hope and belief.
b) free will is an illusion caused by our inability to see physical causes in the brain.
c) all "free" actions are compelled by fear.
d) fear takes over when the ability to reason in logical terms breaks down.

6) Logically speaking, materialism presupposes physical determinism, since free will is:

a) physically caused.
b) spiritually caused.
c) emotionally caused.
d) not caused by external situations.

7) Kant argues that our perspectives on reality are:

a) emotionally determined.
b) physically determined.
c) rationally determined.
d) None of the above.

8) Which of the following were intellectual challenges that Descartes hoped to overcome?

a) To find a place in physical nature for the existence of a non-physical,
   non-quantitative mind.
b) To prove the immortal nature of the soul.
c) To discover appetites and aversions.
d) To reveal physical causes.
e) A and b both.

9) To believe that physical and non-physical realities interact with each other is called

a) materialism
b) idealism
c) parallelism
d) dualistic interactionism

10) To believe that physical and non-physical realities only appear to interact with each other
    is called

a) materialism
b) idealism
c) parallelism
d) dualistic interactionism

Self-Test 3: True/False

1) Some examples of the issues that metaphysics takes up include the existence of God, free will, and the self. T / F

2) We are accustomed to thinking of physical movements and sensations as determined, but tell ourselves they are free. T / F

3) Hobbes states that a free man is not hindered in the ability to do what he has a will to do, and therefore freedom means the ability to do whatever we want. T / F

4) Hobbes also implies that "free" actions are not compelled by fear of the consequences of choosing otherwise. T / F

5) Hume undermines the belief that the future will causally resemble the past by saying that we assume it will. T / F

6) For Kant, appearances or representations are not simply illusions but are connected by empirical laws. T / F

7) For Hume, external factors ultimately determine a person's vision of him or herself as an autonomous individual, and his or her inner emotional states. T / F

8) Descartes held that mind and body are two distinct substances. T / F

9) Ryles claimed that "mind" and "body" were terms of different logical types and thus do not share similar qualities. T/ F

10) U.T. Place claimed that consciousness is a process in the brain, just as lightening is a type of electricity. T / F

III. Essay Questions: For Discussion and Reflection

1) Approaching an awareness of his own forthcoming death, master skeptic David Hume recanted his doubts about the existence of God, a spiritual realm, and other metaphysical matters, admitting that he might have been wrong. Is there knowledge that we might be *able* to obtain but *should* not? Can anyone be rationally certain that the universe is only composed of "mind-atoms" or "atoms of matter"?

2) Because the existence of any non-quantitative immaterial "mind" or immortal soul cannot or has not been proven by speculative philosophy/physics, does this mean that such things do not exist?

3) Assume Hobbes, Ryles and Place are correct about life and the human mind. Can materialist analysis yield a meaning to the deep feelings we experience? Assume a political prisoner suffering greatly in chains for a good cause (such as the overthrow of Nazism) is on the verge of physical death. It's 1942 and he or she has no contact with the outside world (like many concentration camp prisoners). He or she sees no hope for a material victory over the evil, a victory for which he or she is sacrificing his or her life. Recall this person has no way of knowing history's "determined" outcome, and alternative outcomes are always at least theoretically possible. Which philosophers offer our prisoner greater grounds for hope, the materialists or non-materialists? Why?

4) Summarize David Hume's argument against causation found in *Of the Idea of Necessary Connection* on your *Primary Source* CD-ROM. If Hume is correct, explain how your summary can exist without being *caused* by your writing it, or typing it (and of course without someone else doing so).

5) What is Hobbes's view of art as expressed in *Leviathan* on your CD-ROM?

IV. Lecture Companion.

The following lecture note pages can be used to record your instructor's lectures and assignments for this chapter.

Chapter Four: Philosophy of Science

I. Terms for Review

Anomaly: According to Thomas Kuhn, a scientific observation that cannot be explained by the currently accepted paradigm.

Atomism: The cosmological theory which states that all objects are composed of invisible entities called atoms. Lucretius was a defender of this point of view.

Empiricism: The theory of knowledge which states that that ultimate source of knowledge is the senses (seeing, hearing, smelling, tasting, and touching).

Forms: A term used by Francis Bacon to refer to properties of matter.

Normal Science: According to Thomas Kuhn, science conducted within the confines of the currently accepted paradigm.

Observation: The process of collecting data about the universe by using the five senses.

Organon: A method of scientific investigation- it states the logical requirements that are to be use in scientific investigations.

Paradigm: Term used by Thomas Kuhn to refer to an accepted theory of science that serves to guide scientific investigations.

Paradigm Shift: Term used by Thomas Kuhn to describe what happens when an older paradigm is replaced by a new paradigm.

Rationalism: The theory of knowledge which states that the ultimate source of knowledge is reason.

Scientific Facts: The truths that are accepted or revealed about the physical universe.

Scientific Method: The various procedures used by scientists to solve certain problems. It includes such processes as observation, reason, hypothesis formation, testing, experimenting, etc.

Scientific Revolution: A term used by Kuhn to refer to changes of paradigms in science. It can be understood as a change of scientific models where an old model is replaced by an incompatible new model.

Theory Neutral: A term that is applied to observations that are independent of theories about the universe.

II. Practice Tests

Self-Test 1: Definitions/Fill-in

For each sentence below, fill in the blank(s) with the appropriate term(s) or phrase.

1) To Newtonian scientists, observing a physical action that did not have an equal and opposite reaction would be an _____.

2) Because he believed that scientific knowledge began with observation, Francis Bacon was an _____.

3) The_____ whose nature science investigates are familiar everyday characteristics of things we observe with our five senses.

4) For Karl Popper, the line of demarcation between real science and such matters as UFO's and spotting the ghosts of celebrities is_____.

5) Thomas Kuhn may have said that a _____ _____ took place in regards to the science of international affairs in the American national consciousness after the September 11, 2001 terrorist attacks.

6) The switch from Ptolemy's view that the earth was the center of the universe to the Copernican view that the sun was the center of creation is one Kuhn would call a _____.

7) Kuhn counter-argued his critics by claiming that rather than subjective factors causing change in scientific paradigms, _____ methods of analysis cause these sorts of changes.

8) Rationalists such as Newton claim that observation must be guided by_____.

9) For Popper, if a theory cannot be falsified, this may actually not be _____, because it will be weak in its ability to_____ the occurrence and outcome of possible situations.

10) Also in Popper, scientific progress is based on attempts to _____.

Self-Test 2: Multiple Choice

1) Which philosopher below takes an empiricist approach to the scientific method?

a) René Descartes
b) Francis Bacon
c) Thomas Kuhn
d) All of the above

2) Any past traditions in science that continue to serve as guides for future scientific investigations are referred to by Kuhn as:

a) neutral theory.
b) theory neutral.
c) Falsifiable.
d) paradigms.

3) Any outlook or perspective which holds a dominant power as a social institution over a given time period is called (a):

a) neutral theory.
b) theory neutral.
c) falsifiable.
d) paradigm.

4) When one can provide a counterexample of a scientific theory, Popper identifies that theory as:

a) neutral theory.
b) theory neutral.
c) falsifiable.
d) paradigm.

5) Which of the following is NOT a criteria Copi and Cohen identify for rating or evaluating competing scientific theories?

a) Predictive or explanatory power
b) Testability
c) Relevance
d) Social force
e) All of the above are identified as criteria.

6) When rival scientific theories compete for our adoption, the logicians mentioned in question 5 would recommend:

a) continued experimentation.
b) falsification.
c) choosing the most complex explanation.
d) choosing the simplest explanation.
e) None of the above.

7) When we base our choice of theory only upon empirical data, we say we have:

a) an under determination in the approach to the question.
b) an over determination in the approach to the question.
c) social determination in the answer to the question.
d) free will in determining the answer to the debate between theories.

8) Which of the following is NOT a reason Laudan presents as an objective and rational preference in judging the quality of a scientific theory?

a) The theory is internally consistent.
b) The theory correctly makes unexpected or surprising predictions.
c) The theory is well known and exciting to discuss.
d) The theory has been tested against a diverse range of phenomena.

9) Which of the following is one of the implications of Thomas Kuhn's theory?

a) Science is a progressive enterprise.
b) It is possible for observation to be theory neutral.
c) Scientific revolutions never occur.
d) None of the above.

10) According to this thinker, observation is the primary element of the scientific method:

a) René Descartes
b) Francis Bacon
c) Immanuel Kant
d) Thomas Kuhn

Self Test 3: True/False

1) For Popper, when a theory can be made false, we should discard it. T / F

2) Internal consistency is not as important in a theory for Kuhn as it is for Laudan. T / F

3) Empiricism is no longer a relevant criteria for contemporary scientists. T / F

4) Rationalists disregard known theories in their approach to observation of data. T / F

5) Scientific observations that are "theory neutral" stand the "test of time". T / F

6) Revolutions in science are called organons. T / F

7) Good scientific theories should provide a relatively accurate forecast of
future phenomena. T / F

8) For Bacon, one occurrence of a fact or phenomenon was enough to build
a theory. T / F

9) For Kuhn, one factor alone is not enough to cause a crisis in the dominant scientific
paradigm. T / F

10) Observation remains important no matter which theorist of science we consult T / F

III. Essay Questions: For discussion and reflection

1) In terms of the knowledge you can glean from your companion CD, examine Paul
   Henri D'holbach's idea that all decisions we make are simply the result of strong
   environmental impulses on the mind. What about human actions that are
   unpredictable? If the mind is so determined, from whence comes the freedom to
   recognize and challenge the theory of determination by force ?

2) Do scientifically engaged philosophers like Larry Laudan, Karl Popper, Copi and
   Cohen, Isaac Newton, and others share any common criteria for judging effective
   and ineffective scientific theories?

IV. Lecture Companion

The following lecture note pages can be used to record your instructor's lectures and assignments for this chapter.

Chapter Five: Ethical Theory

I. Terms for Review

Act Utilitarianism: A version of utilitarianism that states that each act must be evaluated to see if it will bring about the greatest happiness for the greatest number of people. If the act will bring about the greatest good or happiness for the greatest number of people, the we ought to do that act.

Categorical Imperative: The moral principle of Immanuel Kant that is used to determine the individual's duty.

End: Something is an end if it is regarded as valuable in itself. A family pet that is loved is an end. A person, such as a significant other, is treated as an "end-in-himself" or "herself" if they are loved for who they are, and not used for a selfish purpose.

Ethical Relativism: The view that moral principles vary from individual to individual, from culture to culture, stating that moral principles derive their validity from cultural norms.

Ethics: The branch of philosophy or field of debate that studies morality; the study of how one ought to act, of how moral value judgments are made.

Good Life: A term used by the ancient Greeks to refer to how one should live life. For Plato, it consists of the harmony of the elements of the soul or inner self.

Hedonistic Utility: Moral theory invented by Bentham which states that acts are moral when they produce the greatest amount of pleasure for the agent or agents.

Kantian Ethics: The ethical system developed by Immanuel Kant. It stresses the reason and autonomy of human beings. According to Kant, human beings are worthy of respect and dignity; they are always to be regarded as an ends, never as mere means. The categorical imperative is an important part of Kant's ethical system.

Maxim: In Kantian ethics, this is a candidate for a universal law. If a maxim can be made into a universal law, it is our duty to follow that maxim.

Means: Something is a means if we use it to get something else. If you borrow money from someone and make a promise to pay back the money, if you have no intention of ever paying back the money, you are treating the person as a means, not an end. Also in John Stuart Mill's *Utilitarianism*, the means are the actions undertaken, good or bad, in the name of a goal we can also judge as good or bad. If one breaks a window to save a child from a burning building, the breaking of the window is the means to saving the child.

Morals: As opposed to ethics, morals are simply a particular set of standards for individual behavior concerning right and wrong.

Norm: A standard of behavior; a moral norm is a rule or principle that is used to evaluate behavior as moral or immoral.

Rule Utilitarianism: According to this version of utilitarianism, obeying a rule that will bring about the greatest good result for the greatest number of people is ethical, such as obeying the commandment against stealing.

Utilitarianism: The moral (and social) theory developed by Jeremy Bentham and John Stuart Mill which states that individuals should act in such a way as to create the greatest good for the greatest number.

II. Practice Tests

Self-Test 1: Definitions/Fill-in

For each sentence below, fill in the blank(s) with the appropriate term(s) or phrase.

1) _____: The theory that denies any act is right or wrong.

2) _____ is a branch of applied ethics that is concerned with hard cases in the medical field.

3) If human action was the result of causally determined social and/or natural forces, we could not responsibly expect a person to_____ and_____.

4) In Kantian ethics a _____ is a candidate for a universal law.

5) Doubting the truths of ethics is called_____.

6) Ethical_____ is the view that there is no right and wrong.

7) The view that right and wrong depends upon the culture originating the moral code is called_____.

8) The _____ model favors full disclosure to the patient.

9) The central feminist objection to ethical theory is that because most mainstream ethical theory has been produced by _____, it cannot and/or does not express the _____.

10) Ruth Benedict refers to desirable behavior not in ethical terms but as
_____, and claims it is_____.

Self-Test 2: Multiple Choice

1) Ruth Benedict claims that what mankind prefers to call "morally good" is merely:

a) religiously devout.
b) culturally habitual.
c) materially determined.
d) None of the above.

2) An example of following the Categorical Imperative of Kant would be:

a) stopping at a red light because it makes me happy to do so.
b) stopping at a green light because it causes me pleasure.
c) stopping at a red light because this action produces the greatest social utility.
d) stopping at a red light because safe driving should be a universal law.

3) Which one of these is not a central principle of Kant's theories?

a) Persons are rational creatures, capable of higher level moral reasoning.
b) Persons have intrinsic value and are not to be used.
c) People are the authors of moral laws.
d) The purpose of ethical life is pleasure or eudemonia, happiness.

4) Which Thinker(s) argue that the decision to withhold food and water from a
   patient must be made with the patient's best wishes in mind?

a) Tom Beauchamp
b) James F. Childress
c) Joanne Lynn
d) a and c
e) b and c

5) Which thinker argues that a prohibition against human cloning may be more
   problematic than simply regulating human cloning?

a) Harry Binswanger
b) Paul Ginnetty
c) John F. Kilner
d) Laurence H. Tribe

6) In his *Fundamentals of the Metaphysics of Morals*, Kant says that the ethical principles a free human being forms as supremely practical are:

a) subjective principles designed to help the self feel strong in a hostile situation.
b) emotional principles designed to catharsizes surplus repression.
c) objective principles designed for everyone in all situations.
d) artistic principles designed for negative creativity.

7) In order for an individual to treat humanity as an end and not as a means:

a) reason must be in control of the passions.
b) the passions must be in control of reasons.
c) the world must change.
d) truth must be subjective.

8) If passions command one's personal powers of reason, an individual winds up losing his or her:

a) reason.
b) passions.
c) autonomy or freedom.
d) None of the above.

9) In *A Vindication of the Rights of Women*, Mary Wollstonecraft argued that the real reason for women's oppressed position in 18th century society was not inferior rational or moral powers but:

a) subordination.
b) lack of educational opportunity and restrictive social structures.
c) the predominance of utilitarianism.
d) superior rational and moral powers.

10) Bentham's utilitarian calculations are based upon:

a) total amounts of pleasure.
b) total amounts of pain.
c) benefits and cost analysis.
d) a and b

Self-Test 3: True/False

1) Feminists argue for the reevaluation of all social institutions from a different paradigm that takes into account the experiences and philosophical insights of women. T / F

2) David Hume argues that human behavior is a result of our desires; that desires are really what motivate us to act. T / F

3) Engels rooted the first class opposition in society between serfs and their lord. T / F

4) Simone de Beauvoir was the first philosopher to address the social inequality between the sexes. T / F

5) Modern philosophers seek to have their findings consistent with contemporary empiricist moral psychology. T / F

6) Alison Jaggar argues that traditional Western Philosophy is deeply concerned with women's interests. T / F

7) Plato, considered the "father of utilitarianism", developed utilitarianism in hopes of reforming social and legal injustices of the day. T / F

8) Feminist theorists focus on social processes rather than individual subjects. T / F

9) Jaggar would agree with Kant on the existence of an objective moral reality independent of perceiving minds. T / F

10) Ethical skepticism denies that anyone can have any certainty about moral issues. T / F

III. Essay Questions: For discussion and reflection

1) Re-examine Aristotle's writings on ethics from your companion *Primary Source* CD-ROM and other primary sources if necessary, discuss whether or not "virtue" is a term only describing human behavior or an ideal state of affairs. Is virtue only one characteristic of an individual or are there several categories exemplifying virtue including "courage", "generosity" and others?

2) If a government was to choose to conduct itself according to a set of laws derived from Ruth Benedict's ethical relativism and Jean Jacques-Rousseau's sentimentalism (each of these are found on the *Primary Source* CD-ROM), what kind of social order or lack thereof would result? Whose feelings claim authority?

3) Also on the subject of Aristotle, as you familiarize yourself with his concept of happiness, (from the *Primary Source* CD-ROM and other original sources as necessary), discuss whether or not "happiness", a concept later borrowed by John Stuart Mill, refers only or primarily to the body, to a physical satisfaction of needs?

4) Is the sphere of moral reasoning exclusive of matters regarding intimate and family relations? How do the points of view included in *About Philosophy* on cloning and same-sex marriage prove that it is not?

5) From your CD rom *Primary Source*, read again Dr. Martin Luther King, Jr.'s Letter from Birmingham Jail. In his accurate arguments demonstrating the injustice of segregation and the need for nonviolent direct action, how is King able to bring together empiricism, subjective moral insights and the existence of an objective reality to which universal laws apply?

6) Define applied ethics and medical ethics.

IV. Lecture Companion

The following lecture note pages can be used to record your instructor's lectures and assignments for this chapter.

Chapter Six: Social and Political Philosophy

I. Terms for Review

Alienation of Labor: The term used by Karl Marx to describe the relation of the laborer to the product produced. Human beings need meaningful work, but the work that is found in capitalism does not satisfy this need of the workers.

Anarchist: One who denies that the state has the right to rule; the denial of the legitimacy of the state.

Argument: Reasoning involving a conclusion that is supported by premises.

Capitalism: The private ownership of business and industry which produce goods that are priced and marketed on the basis of supply and demand.

Color Line: The difference of attitudes and treatment that exists between whites and other people of color.

Conservative: A social-political view that emphasizes the status quo and custom or tradition.

End: Used in the sense of a goal; having intrinsic value.

Irrational: Contrary to reason; involving a contradiction.

Laissez-Faire: The system of free market exchanges, with an absolute minimum of government control, which the nineteenth century liberals believed would result in the most efficient use of resources and the greatest material well-being for society.

Liberal: A social-political view that emphasizes personal liberty and individual freedom rather than equality.

Marxism: The social-political view of Karl Marx that stresses personal and social equality and argues that capitalism is unjust, attempting to remedy those injustices through worker ownership of the means of production.

Rational: Based on or appealing to reason.

Social Contract: A concept used by political philosophers to explain the legitimacy of the state; it is a voluntary and binding agreement between an individual and others to accept certain social-political conditions as a basis for the common good of all.

Socialism: The social-political theory wherein the members of society collectively own the resources and determine how they will be used.

State: The collections of those who construct, issue and enforce laws on others living within a given area.

Tacit Consent: A term used to explain how later generations of citizens become parties to the social contract; the idea that a person through his behavior has given his word to obey certain principles or laws.

Utilitarianism: The view that society should produce the greatest amount of happiness for the greatest number of people.

II. Practice Tests

Self-Test 1: Definitions/Fill-in

For each sentence below, fill in the blank(s) with the appropriate term(s) or phrase.

1) John Stuart Mill would call reading a text by Plato a _____ sort of pleasure and getting inebriated a _____ sort of pleasure.

2) Rather than suggesting that a rational natural force or "invisible hand" of the marketplace will direct the economic activities of consumers, Mill argued that_____ or _____ tastes and preferences govern consumers or actors in the marketplace, so their behavior isn't _____.

3) The 18th century philosopher who advocated pure laissez-faire was _____.

4) The two motives that can be predicted in the marketplace is that actors will_____and_____.

5) "Liberal" in political philosophy comes from the same Latin root as _____, and 18th/19th century "liberals" were concerned with giving individuals in the marketplace greater _____ from government interference.

6) Jean-Jacques Rousseau claims that the legitimacy of the state is based on_____.

7) Marx divides society into _____ and _____.

8) The most important layer of society's material base is what Marx called the_____.

9) Factories, technology, machinery and expertise in labor are the _____.

10) Subjects such as art, religion and philosophy are referred to by Marx as the _____ of society.

Self-Test 2: Multiple Choice

1) Karl Marx's claim is that capitalism:

a) operates according to rational natural laws.
b) should be unfettered by governmental regulations.
c) is based on a repressive and illogical set of relationships.
d) should be limited to protect interest-groups' rights.

2) Charles Mills would contend that capitalism:

a) operates according to rational natural laws.
b) should be unfettered by governmental regulations.
c) is based on a repressive and illogical set of relationships.
d) should be limited to protect interest-groups' rights.
e) a) and b)

3) On the other hand, John Stuart Mill and Adam Smith might contend that capitalism:

a) operates according to rational natural laws.
b) should be unfettered by governmental regulations.
c) is based on a repressive and illogical set of relationships.
d) should be limited to protect interest-groups' rights.
e) a) and b)

4) Jean-Jacques Rousseau refers to the decision of the citizens of a republic to set aside their private and partisan concerns and collectively aim at a greater good as:

a) sentimentalism.
b) capitalism.
c) proletarianism.
d) the general will.
e) the laissez-faire.

5) The ruling class in Marxist philosophy gains control over the means of production by:

a) the general will.
b) laissez-faire.
c) force of arms.
d) the social relationships of production.

6) The fact that capitalists own the factories forms an example of what Marx calls the:

a) means of production.
b) relationships of production.
c) proletariat.
d) bourgeoisie.

7) Pluralists believe that:

a) government should not interfere with natural capitalism.
b) workers should control the means of production.
c) special interest groups are vital to protecting democratic representation between elections.
d) affirmative action is a racial contract.

8) The example of popular movies about Africa is evoked to illustrate that:

a) government should not interfere with natural capitalism.
b) traditional social contracts do not include the interest or consent of nonwhites.
c) special interest groups are vital to protecting democratic representation between elections.
d) affirmative action is a social contract.

9) The relationship of economic activity to academic activity in Marxism is that:

a) academic activity forms the base of economic activity.
b) political relationships in the social contract form the base of both activities.
c) these activities form the means of production such as the factory.
d) economic activity is at the base of other relationships in society such as philosophy or other studies.

10) One reason why a Marxist country would not support organized religion is that:

a) communist states are materialistic atheists.
b) churches do not return value to the collective; they share in the portion of the product taken by the rulers.
c) Marx himself was a materialist.
d) None of the above.

11) The fundamental division in society for Marx was between:

a) racial groups.
b) ethnic groups.
c) bourgeoisie and proletariat.
d) Western and Non-western.
e) theist and atheist.

Self-Test 3: True/False

1) An anarchist believes that no state has any right to rule and that governmental authority is illegitimate and undesirable. T / F

2) Adam Smith would have accepted the label "liberal" to describe his economic policies. T / F

3) John Stuart Mill's version of utilitarianism has a less precise definition of pleasures and their value than does Bentham. T / F

4) For Marx, the bourgeoisie are oppressed in their struggle for justice and social equality. T / F

5) Marx never varied his theories over time and always advocated violent revolution. T / F

6) Earl Latham was not an advocate of the theory of pluralism. T / F

7) Alienation means that workers are unhappy both at their jobs and at leisure. T / F

8) Rousseau was suspicious of representational forms of activity such as government. T / F

9) Charles Mills suggests that the social contract theory, forged in the 18th century, concealed the realities of racism and slavery that we still call into philosophical question today. T / F

10) Mills thinks European humanism represented all humans as equals. T / F

III. Essay Questions: For discussion and reflection

1) Summarize Stanley Fish's discussion of affirmative action in the first article on this topic. How convincing do you find his case in terms of pluralism or other political theories we have examined in this chapter?

2) In John Locke's *The Second Treatise of Government*, (found on your *Primary Source* CD-ROM) human rights to free and equal treatment are rooted in nature. What are the implications of Locke's idea of nature on the political theory of communism as we have seen it practiced in recent history?

3) Do you find any conflict between the role of special interest groups and the impartiality of mass utilitarianism that John Stuart Mill advocates on the CD in his text *Utilitarianism*? Do special interest group needs conflict with "the greatest good for the greatest number"?

4) In Chapter Seven of Adam Smith's *An Inquiry Into the Nature and Causes of the Wealth of Nations*, (also on your CD), how does Smith define the value of the labor? Compare and contrast his approach to the question of labor to Marx's ideas on labor's value?

IV. Lecture Companion

The following lecture note pages can be used to record your instructor's lectures and assignments for this chapter.

Chapter Seven: Philosophy of Art

I. Terms for Review

Aesthetics: The branch of philosophy that deals with the study of art. "Philosophy of art" is used as a synonym for the word "aesthetics."

Appearance: A metaphysical term that refers to how things seem to be as opposed to how they really are. (Note: The terms "appearance" and "reality" are often used together as an important metaphysical distinction.)

Artistic Alienation: Defined by Marcuse as the attempt to consciously transcend everyday experience to a new paradigm wherein imagining a more egalitarian future, and just social order is possible.

Catharsis: Aristotle uses the term to describe the effect on us of powerful dramatic performances. By watching a play that features events arousing fear and pity within us, he thought, we are purged of those emotions, leaving the theatre liberated or cleansed.

Forms: A metaphysical term used by Plato to refer to non-material, eternal and changeless entities that constitute reality. Examples of forms are Beauty, Justice the Good, etc.

Instrumental Value: The worth something has due to its use.

Intrinsic Value: The inherent worth something has, for the sake of itself and not as a means to an end.

Metaphysics: The branch of philosophy that studies the question of what is real; the study of the nature of reality.

Necessary Repression: The suppression of certain desires, feelings, and thoughts in order to survive at a given stage of society.

Repression: A Freudian term that refers to a mental regulation of strong desires, thoughts and ideas that are considered anti-social.

Romanticism: The late 18th century movement that rebelled against the elements of Neoclassicism; it emphasized creative imagination and subjectivity as the basis of truth in art.

Surplus Repression: The excess or unnecessary suppression of desires that is the result of the domination of those in power.

II. Practice Tests

Self-Test 1: Definitions/Fill-in

For each sentence below, fill in the blank(s) with the appropriate term(s) or phrase.

1) The branch of philosophy that deals with the study of art is called _____.

2) The ability to tell between what seems to be right, good, accurate, or true and what seems to be wrong, false, misleading, or fallacious is_____.

3) The ethical problem in Plato's Gorgias is that Gorgias's students tend to do as he _____ and not as he _____.

4) A theme of the dialogue Gorgias is the danger of believing that there are no_____.

5) Plato criticizes the object of a work of art, such as the image of a chair in a painting, because it is simply a _____ of a_____ of a real thing.

6) Plato criticizes tragic poets because they _____ emotions which threaten to _____.

7) Aristotle's defense of art and poetry, called _____, claims that art enables us to grasp the _____ within particular material objects.

8) Because Aristotle holds that universal _____ are embodied within _____ _____, art allows us access to these truths.

9) Aristotle would say that our attention should be focused _____ upon particular material things.

10) The effect tragedy has upon us of cleansing or purging negative emotions is what Aristotle calls_____.

Self-Test 2: Multiple Choice

1) Herbert Marcuse argues that because great art is so negative, destructive and irrational, it is:

a) a worthless endeavor.
b) a provocation of harmful emotions.
c) a catharsis.
d) a valuable element in human life.

2) According to your text, part of the problem with socially engaging art used to protest in America is that it:

a) provokes a catharsis.
b) is reabsorbed into harmless mainstream culture.
c) does not protest stridently enough.
d) is fundamentally negative, destructive and irrational.

3) Forcibly pushing out consciousness of desires, wishes, thoughts, or feelings the mind considers bad or negative is called by Freud:

a) catharsis
b) sublimation
c) repression
d) oppression

4) Redirecting sexual or aggressive energies into socially or morally acceptable channels is called, by Freud,:

a) catharsis.
b) sublimation.
c) repression.
d) oppression.

5) Marcuse claims that we carry over from our infancy:

a) sublimation.
b) catharsis.
c) desires for immediate and total gratification.
d) fears and doubts.

6) Marcuse is famous for transforming Freud's claim about repression by:

a) disproving repression.
b) dividing into necessary and surplus repression.
c) transforming it into sublimation.
d) None of the above.

7) Surplus repression is:

a) necessary for survival.
b) generated by oppressive power.
c) a catalyst for the creation of great art in Marcuse.
d) None of the above.
e) b) and c).

8) Human progress for Marcuse has the impact of:

a) eliminating surplus repression.
b) decreasing the amount of necessary repression.
c) generating great art.
d) a) and b).

9) For Marcuse, our repressed subconscious negative thoughts.

a) form a surplus.
b) are necessary.
c) exist as a permanent psychic pool or source of opposition to society.
d) None of the above.

10) Marcuse argued that art has a valuable role to play in reducing:

a) negative repression.
b) surplus repression of a society.
c) desire.
d) boredom.

Self -Test 3: True/False

1) Marcuse argues that we can totally eliminate all forms of repression. T / F

2) Transcendence means the same thing for Marcuse and Plato. T / F

3) Art does not need to keep our hopes for a better world alive in Marcuse. T / F

4) "Mimesis" or the representation of reality is a negative thing in both Aristotle and Plato. T / F

5) Plato values poetry more highly than does Aristotle. T / F

6) Marcuse values the negation of the accepted social order that he feels great art embodies. T / F

7) "Found art" consists of ordinary objects raised to the level of art. T / F

8) An example of "found art" is "R Mutt" by Marcel Duchamp. T / F

9) Danto's art theories are parallel to Thomas Kuhn's paradigms. T / F

10) We constitute or create the category of "great art" according to Danto. T / F

III. Essay Questions: For discussion and reflection

1) In Aristotle's *Poetics*, found on your companion CD-ROM, the ancient philosopher identifies a certain character type who he says must serve as the hero in a tragic drama. What would Marcuse or other Marxist critics of art have to say about Aristotle's choice of tragic protagonist?

2) Marcuse insists that art must be negative to have a progressive social function. Can you think of any examples of art positively produced or received that served such a function, even temporarily?

3) In Plato's *Republic* part 3, the theory of art that *About Philosophy* refers to in Chapter Five is discussed. In Plato's *Symposium*, what topic does Socrates agree is suitable for artistic representation? Does this choice of topic contradict Plato's criticism of tragic poetry as arousing strong and dangerous emotions?

IV. Lecture Companion

The following lecture note pages can be used to record your instructor's lectures and assignments for this chapter.

Chapter Eight: Philosophy of Religion

I. Terms for Review

A Posteriori: A Latin term used in philosophy to refer to knowledge that comes after experience or is based on experience. The cosmological and teleological (design) arguments are classified as *a posteriori* because they are based on observation or experience.

A Priori: A Latin Term used in philosophy to refer to knowledge that is prior to or not based on experience. The ontological argument is classified as *a priori* because it is based on reason, not on observation.

Analogy: A form of reasoning in which there is a comparison of the characteristics of two things that are similar in some way. The idea is that if the first thing has a certain characteristic, then the second thing, which is similar to the first thing, must also have that characteristic.

Analytic: A classification term for statements in which the subject term contains the predicate term. For example. A bachelor is an unmarried male. (The predicate "unmarried male" is contained in the subject "bachelor.")

Argument: A process of reasoning in which premises are offered in support of a conclusion. The idea is that the conclusion follows logically from the premises, if the argument is valid.

Contingent Being: Existence that is dependent, and that is neither necessary nor impossible. A being with this kind of existence is dependent upon something else for its existence. (Example: A fish is dependent upon water.)

Existentialism: A philosophical view that focuses on the question of the nature, the meaning, and the purpose of human existence. Søren Kierkegaard is generally considered to be the founder of Existentialism.

Leap of Faith: An expression used by Kierkegaard to refer to the unquestioned acceptance of God's promise of salvation.

Natural Theology: What we can know about God through using our reason and looking at Nature.

Necessary Being: A Being which cannot not exist. Such a Being must exist. It has never been created, and it cannot be destroyed. A Necessary Being is the opposite of something whose existence is impossible—such as a four-sided triangle.

Objective: In accordance with reality, existing independently of the differences of opinion between perceiving subjects.

<u>Problem of Evil</u>: The problem of explaining the existence of evil in a universe created by an omnipotent, omniscient, benevolent God.

<u>Revelation</u>: A theological term that refers to the process of God giving to humankind certain information or knowledge. Sacred scripture is an example of revelation.

<u>Revealed Theology</u>: What we can know about God through revelation.

<u>Subjective</u>: Dependent upon the subject—a matter of opinion.

<u>Synthetic</u>: A classification term for statements in which the subject term does not contain the predicate term within its basic definition.

<u>Tautology</u>: A statement that is true due to semantics, in other words, the conceptual meaning of the words. This is an example of a tautology: Either today is July 1, or today is not July 1. A tautology is always true.

<u>Ontological Argument</u>: The attempt to prove the existence of God by starting with nothing more than the concept of the most perfect being. The argument is extremely controversial and has been rejected as invalid by many religious philosophers, including the leading medieval proponent of the Cosmological Argument, St. Thomas Aquinas.

II. Practice Tests

Self-Test 1: Definitions/Fill-in

For each sentence below, fill in the blank(s) with the appropriate term(s) or phrase.

1) The _____ is the argument that states that a _____ mover must have set the rest of the universe in motion.

2) St. Thomas Aquinas also argues that because every event is caused, there must have been a _____ _____ cause that everyone names God.

3) _____ is the philosophical doctrine which states that our being as subjective individuals or _____, such as our purpose, is more important than what we have in common objectively with other human beings, such as our ears.

4) The philosophy defined by your correct answer to question 3 above is said to begin with the philosopher _____.

5) A group of pious Danish citizens who would listen smugly to Sunday preaching but wouldn't let it change their point of view or lifestyle would be the _____.

6) Because logical reason is inadequate to the task of supporting our belief in God's promises, according to Kierkegaard we must make an emotional _____ of _____.

7) The fact that the idea of a being which is the greatest possible thing possible must exist in order to be the greatest forms the basis of the_____ argument for the existence of God.

8) The opposite view of the cosmological argument of "first cause" is called the infinite _____.

9) Kant opposes the ontological argument by stating that_____.

10) The fact that an innocent person could die under a dictatorship is an example of the _____ of _____.

Self-Test 2: Multiple Choice

1) While the Roman Catholic Church would emphasize performing "good works," such as receiving the sacraments, Pietism, the Christianity of Kant and Kierkegaard, placed a heavier emphasis upon:

a) passion for the Cross.
b) unconditioned faith in God.
c) philosophizing and prayer.
d) obedience to the Church's leaders.

2) In his writing entitled "Concluding Unscientific Postscript", found on your *Primary Source* CD-ROM, Søren Kierkegaard characterizes God's relationship to man as:

a) an objective set of facts that can be memorized.
b) an all-determining "Divine Will."
c) an unhappy lover longing to be with his beloved woman.
d) the governor of a democratic state of man's soul.
e) None of the above.

3) As opposed to Hegelian scientists who argued that God was a logical and objectively demonstrable reality, Kierkegaard took the position that absolute Truth was:

a) objective.
b) subjective.
c) tautology.
d) ontological.

4) According to Kierkegaard, since man cannot think his way to God like Socrates resolving a question, God bridged the gap by:

a) sending Jesus as a means to personal salvation.
b) dictating His Word as the Bible.
c) enlightening our minds with knowledge.
d) giving us the idea of a Savior.

5) In his written text "Natural Theology" found on the *Primary Source* CD, William Paley's first argument is that we would still believe that the watch we discovered had a maker even if:

a) we had never witnessed a watch being made.
b) we did not know anyone who'd made a watch.
c) we couldn't ourselves make a watch and/or had no idea how to do so.
d) All of the above.

6) The reading, "Concerning Natural Religion", found on your *Primary Source* CD, David Hume accounts for our imperfect world by raising the possibility that:

a) God is a mere baby whose imperfect creation is a rough draft or "rude essay".
b) God had become too old or "superannuated" to create a better world when this one was made.
c) God is an inferior deity mocked by superior deities.
d) all of these ideas are possibilities.

7) Christians apparently derive their beliefs about God from:

a) Reason
b) Thought
c) Revelation
d) truth
e) a) and c)

8) The fact that one hundred real dollars would make a merrier holiday for most of us than the idea of one hundred dollars forms:

a) Anselm's challenge to atheism.
b) Aquinas's challenge to Anselm.
c) Hume's challenge to the argument from design.
d) Kant's challenge to the ontological argument.

9) Hume argues that:

a) if God is willing to prevent evil, but not able, then he is not omnipotent.
b) if God is able to prevent evil, but not willing, then he is not benevolent.
c) God is benevolent and omnipotent.
d) God is all-good and not evil.
e) a) and b)

10) Free will helps to account for the reality of evil by suggesting:

a) God is only a figment of the will.
b) without free will, good and evil would be meaningless because our actions would be robotically determined.
c) Neither a) nor b).
d) that free will, along with evil, is only an illusion of aversion and desire.
e) a) and b)

Self-Test 3: True/False

1) The Kierkegaardian "leap of faith" can be explained through rational analysis or logical materialist argument. T / F

2) There are no counterarguments to the ontological case for God. T / F

3) In response to the argument from design, Hume reflects that we do not know enough about the universe to discern the nature of the Creator, or indeed if there is one. T / F

4) The ontological argument proposes God as a being that is contingent, not necessary. T / F

5) Omnipotence means that God is all knowing. T / F

6) Both Kierkegaard and Thomas Aquinas propose logical and rational approaches to the subject of God's existence. T / F

7) Kant does not object that the ontological argument only demonstrates analytic statements where the predicate term relating to God is contained within the subject. T / F

8) Kierkegaard compares the leap of faith to an episode from the life of Moses in the Bible. T / F

9) Mystical experiences of God require logically demonstrable proofs of God's existence. T / F

10) Counterarguments for the cosmological argument reflect the limits of human knowledge. T / F

III. Essay Questions: For discussion and reflection.

1. Reread William James's writings on Mysticism on the *Primary Source* CD-ROM. What does James suggest about the superiority of the mystic's approach to God, as opposed to the rationalistic philosophical arguments for the existence of God?

2. From Aquinas's *Summa Theologica* (Found on the *Primary Source* CD-ROM), how does he deal with the problem of evil? Use an example from your own life if possible, to illustrate how a good can come out of an evil.

3. Read Anselm's *Proslogion* also from the CD. To what degree is the author praying rather than performing a logical analysis ? If you are an atheist, is there anything in your life you feel as passionately about proving to others as Anselm does about proving God is real?

4. Re-examine Kant's *Fundamental Principles of the Metaphysics of Morals* CD selection. Looking especially at Kant's guide to actions and his statement on practical love, can we counter-argue the idea that Pietists before Kierkegaard were justified in doing nothing with their Christian faith ?

IV. Lecture Companion

The following lecture note pages can be used to record your instructor's lectures and assignments for this chapter.

Self-Test Answer Key for Chapter One

Test 1: Definitions/ Fill-in

1) irony
2) Western Philosophy
3) objective
4) dialogue
5) Water
6) Philosophy
7) "the unexamined life"
8) Plato, Academy, Athens, 387
9) universal
10) the truth
11) universal
12) South Africa, apartheid
13) the human committments
14) double consciousness

Test 2: Multiple Choice

1) b
2) d
3) d
4) c
5) c
6) c
7) c
8) b
9) c
10) c
11) a
12) d
13) a
14) d
15) c

Test 3: True / False

1) T
2) F
3) T
4) T
5) T

6) T
7) T
8) F
9) F
10) T

Self-Test Answer Key for Chapter Two

Test 1: Definitions / Fill-in

1) Empirical skepticism
2) skepticism, solipsism
3) doubt as much as possible any belief or claim assumed to be true
4) own existence
5) Contradiction
6) Excluded Middle
7) God
8) rasa, blank, slate, written
9) bound together in a unity by being all contained in one consciousness
10) skepticism or empirical skepticism

Test 2: Multiple Choice

1) b
2) d
3) c
4) b
5) d
6) d
7) d
8) c
9) b
10) b

Test 3: True/False

1) F
2) T
3) T
4) F
5) F
6) T
7) T
8) F
9) F
10) T

Self-Test Answer Key for Chapter Three

Test 1: Definitions/Fill-in

1) after, metaphysics, fundamental aspects
2) material
3) Dualism
4) nonmaterial objects or states
5) appetites
6) consciousness
7) explaining exactly what the relationship is between our minds and physical bodies in space. Three questions are associated with this problem: a) Do minds and bodies interact with one another? b) Can minds really know anything at all about bodies? And c) What is the special relationship between my mind and my body?
8) Substance
9) dualistic interaction
10) identity theories

Test 2: Multiple Choice

1) b
2) c
3) a
4) c
5) b
6) a
7) c
8) e
9) d
10) c

Test 3: True/False

All are true

Self-Test Answer Key for Chapter Four

Test 1: Definition/Fill-in

1) anomaly
2) empiricist
3) forms
4) falsifiability
5) paradigm shift
6) scientific revolution
7) rational
8) theory
9) weakness, predict
10) falsify

Test 2: Multiple Choice

1) b
2) d
3) d
4) c
5) d
6) e
7) a
8) c
9) d
10) b

Test 3: True/ False

1) F
2) F
3) F
4) F
5) T
6) F
7) T
8) F
9) F
10) T

Self-Test Answer Key for Chapter Five

Test 1: Definition/ Fill-in

1) Ethical nihilism
2) medical ethics
3) resist temptation, hold to the moral law
4) maxim
5) ethical skepticism
6) nihilism
7) ethical relativism
8) autonomy
9) men, experiences and insight of women.
10) normal or normality, habitual

Test 2: Multiple Choice

1) b
2) d
3) d
4) e
5) d
6) c
7) a
8) c
9) b
10) d

Test 3: True/False

1) T
2) T
3) F
4) F
5) T
6) F
7) F
8) T
9) F
10) T

Self-Test Answer-Key for Chapter Six

Test 1: Definition/ Fill-in

1) higher, lower
2) habit, custom, calculable
3) Adam Smith
4) seek to maximize profits or enjoyments; make use of the available information in a rational attempt to achieve that maximization
5) liberation, freedom
6) the social contract
7) the bourgeoisie, the proletariat
8) means of production
9) forces of production
10) superstructures

Test 2: Multiple Choice

1) c
2) d
3) e
4) d
5) c
6) b
7) c
8) b
9) d
10) b
11) c

Test 3: True/False

1) T
2) T
3) F
4) F
5) F
6) F
7) T
8) T
9) T
10) F

Self-Test Answer Key for Chapter Seven

Test 1: Definition/ Fill-in

1) aesthetics
2) reason
3) says, does
4) universal moral principles
5) representation, image
6) stimulate and strengthen, undermine reason
7) The Poetics, universal or universal truths
8) forms, material things
9) even more intently
10) catharsis

Test 2: Multiple Choice

1) d
2) b
3) c
4) b
5) c
6) b
7) e
8) d
9) c
10) b

Test 3: True/False

1) F
2) F
3) F
4) F
5) F
6) T
7) T
8) T
9) T
10) T

Self-Test Answer Key for Chapter Eight

Test 1: Definition/ Fill in

1) cosmological argument, first
2) efficient first
3) Existentialism, existence
4) Søren Kierkegaard
5) bourgeoisie
6) leap of faith
7) ontological
8) regress
9) existence is not a proper predicate
10) problem of evil

Test 2: Multiple Choice

1) b
2) c
3) b
4) a
5) d
6) d
7) e
8) d
9) e
10) b

Test 3: True/ False

1) F
2) F
3) T
4) F
5) F
6) F
7) F
8) F
9) F
10) T